Hi, boys and girls!
Come with us as we find out

What *Really* Happened to the Dinosaurs?

What *REALLY* Happened
to the
DINOSAURS?

First printing: November 1990
Thirteenth printing, June 2003

ISBN: 0-89051-159-4

Library of Congress Cataloging in Publication Data
        Chong, Jonathan, 1956 -
        Ham, Ken, B.App.Sc., Dip.Ed., 1951 -
        Morris, John D., Ph.D., 1946 -

        1. Dinosauria — Juvenile literature
        2. Paleontology

Rewritten from an earlier edition authored by Mark Dinsmore.

Printed in China

Please visit our website for other great titles:
www.masterbooks.net

Dedicated to:

Our Own Dear Children,

Nathan	Chara
Renee	Tim
Danielle	Beth
Jeremy	
Kristel	

and all the other boys and girls who will read this book. May each of you, at an early age, place your faith in our Lord Jesus Christ, our great Creator and Savior.

Ken Ham and *John Morris*

My American Mother,

Mrs. Clara Deyo
I appreciate you all the days of my life.

Jonathan Chong

5

Meet Tracker John and D. J.

Hi, boys and girls. My name is Tracker John. My little dinosaur friend and I welcome you to one of the most interesting places in the world, the Institute for Creation Research (ICR). Don't be scared. Dino Jr. (just call him D. J. for short) is a friendly dinosaur. He is a psittacosaurus (sit-uh-ko-SAWR-us). These dinosaurs are often called parrot dinosaurs because of their noses. D. J. and I would like to show you what *really* happened to the dinosaurs!

Many special scientists work here at ICR. We call these scientists special because they are *creation* scientists. They believe what the Bible says. Each day they learn more about how God made the world with all its different animals and plants, and some of these scientists have spent many years studying about dinosaurs. We come here a lot to learn about dinosaurs, so join us as we see some of the many things that ICR scientists have learned about one of God's mightiest creations—the dinosaurs.

PART 1
IN THE BEGINNING

In the Bible, right at the beginning, is a special book called Genesis. In this Book God tells us how He made the world and all the plants and animals in six days. This means He must have made lions, kangaroos, birds, dogs, and, yes—dinosaurs!

You have lots of questions, don't you? I can hear you saying, "But Tracker John, how do we know dinosaurs existed?" "Where are they now?" "Why did God make them?" "When did God make them?" "Are there dinosaurs living today?" I love it when boys and girls ask me questions about dinosaurs, because the ICR scientists have taught D. J. and me how to find the answers.

Do you see what D. J. and I are looking at? That's right, footprints! Great big footprints that were made by a great big animal with great big feet! What animal do you think made these footprints? You guessed it, a great big dinosaur! Even though dinosaurs may not be alive today, we still are able to learn many things about them.

9

What is a Dinosaur?

The word dinosaur means "terrible lizard." When dinosaur bones were first found, about 150 years ago, scientists saw that they were different from animals alive today. But, because they looked a lot like huge lizards, they called them "dinosaurs," which means *"terrible* lizards"! Since that time, scientists all over the world have found pieces of bones and sometimes even whole skeletons of dinosaurs. Some of them were giants, but some of them were small, often no bigger than a chicken. However, they were not like the lizards we see today. They had a different type of skeleton.

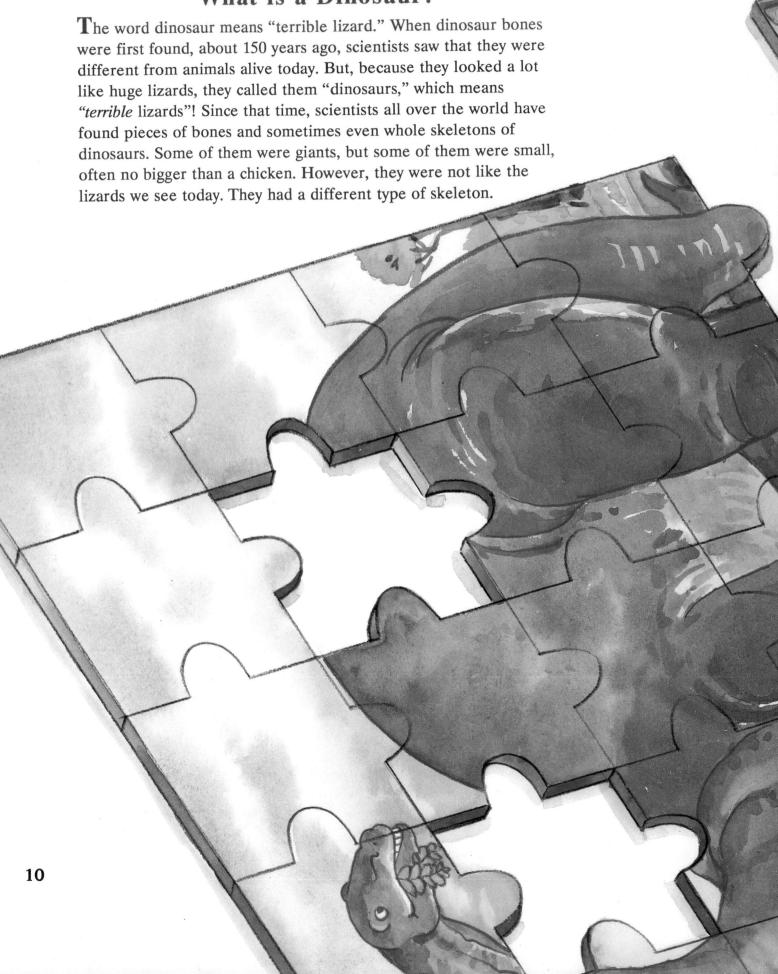

10

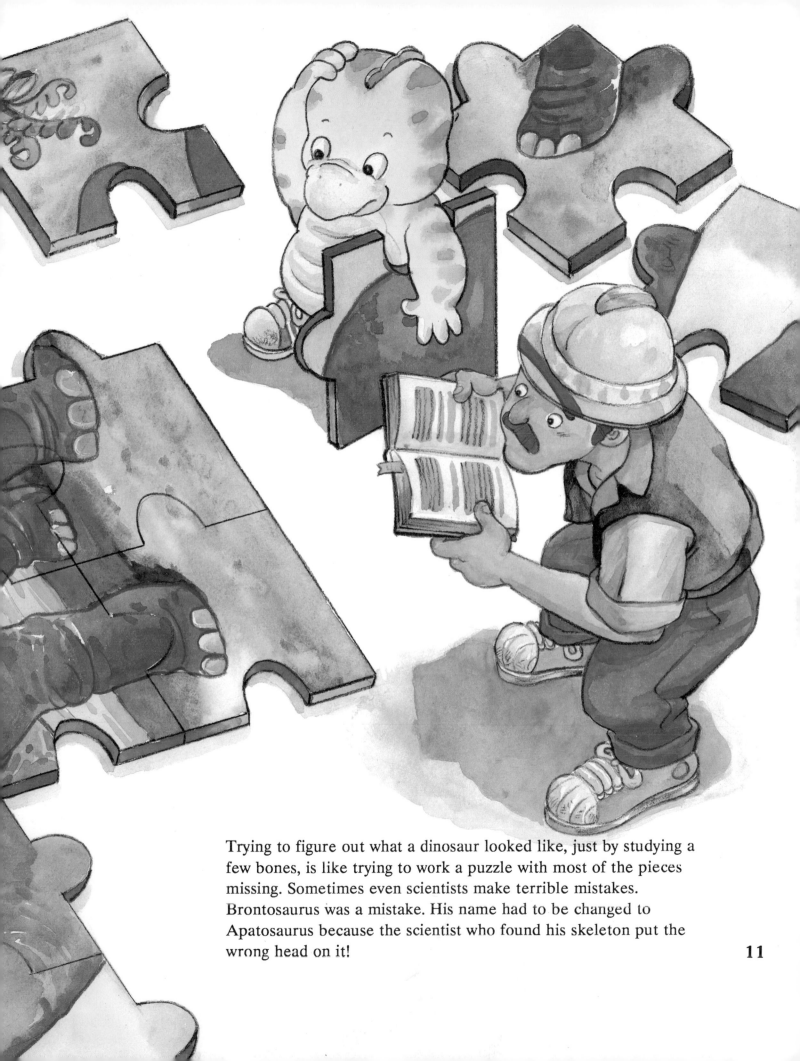

Trying to figure out what a dinosaur looked like, just by studying a few bones, is like trying to work a puzzle with most of the pieces missing. Sometimes even scientists make terrible mistakes. Brontosaurus was a mistake. His name had to be changed to Apatosaurus because the scientist who found his skeleton put the wrong head on it!

When Did Dinosaurs Live?

What's this? Dinosaurs and people together? Some scientists think that dinosaurs lived millions of years ago, long before humans lived on the earth. But the Bible tells us the real story. The Bible tells us that God made the dinosaurs on day six of Creation week, only thousands of years ago. Do you know who God also made on day six to care for the world? Adam and Eve, the first two humans, our great, great, great, great. . .grandparents. Do you know what this means? Dinosaurs must have lived at the same time as Adam and Eve. Wow! Wouldn't that have been exciting!

How Big Were the Dinosaurs?

Look at this picture of Apatosaurus. He is bigger than the ICR building! I think the reason we love dinosaurs is because when we see skeletons of the great big ones, they look like great big monsters. And children love stories about monsters, don't they?

Did you know that the Bible tells us about a huge monster that lived at the time of Job? The monster's name was Behemoth, who ate grass like an ox, had powerful hind legs and a strong belly. His tail was as big around as a large tree, and his bones were strong like metal. He lived in a swampy marsh area, but when the river would flood, Behemoth was not bothered at all. No one could capture him when he was on guard, and he could not be tamed. He was the largest of all land animals (see Job, Chapter 40).

Could this huge animal God was describing be an elephant? No. An elephant's tail isn't big like a tree, is it? Behemoth was the largest land animal God made. Can you guess what animal this might be? You are right. It's probably a dinosaur! God made the dinosaurs and they lived at the same time as Adam and Eve, and they were still living in the time of Job. This *is* getting exciting, isn't it?

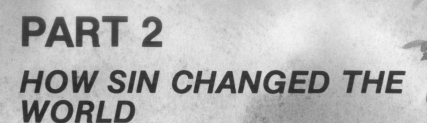

PART 2

HOW SIN CHANGED THE WORLD

When God first created dinosaurs, He told them that they could only eat plants (Genesis 1:30). Now, I know what you are thinking. Some pictures show dinosaurs eating meat, and dinosaur fossil teeth look like they could eat meat. No one really knows for sure, but eventually some dinosaurs probably did eat meat.

But remember, when they were first created, dinosaurs were plant eaters. What happened to God's created world to change it? That's right, sin. The Bible says that Adam and Eve sinned when they disobeyed God. And disobedience is sin, isn't it?

The Bible says that "the wages (or punishment) of sin is death" (Romans 6:23). Ever since Adam and Eve sinned, animals and people have been dying. Sin is a horrible thing. Sin ruined God's beautiful Creation (Genesis 3:14–19).

16

Imagine what a beautiful world it must have been before sin. Beautiful plants like these must have covered the earth. Many of the creatures God made grew much larger than they do today. There were even giant snails and giant dragonflies.

18

D. J. is not so sure he would want to be close to a giant dragonfly. But D. J. and I would have been friends with all the animals, including the dinosaurs, just as Adam was. If Adam had not sinned, death would not have been in the world, and friendly dinosaurs would still be around. Sin is such a terrible thing, isn't it?

Did Dinosaurs Become Violent?

The Bible tells us that because of sin the world soon became wicked and evil. Almost everyone hated God. People fought with each other. Maybe some of the dinosaurs fought and killed each other and people, too. That would not have been a very nice world to live in (Genesis 6:13).

But there was one man who loved and obeyed God. His name was Noah. He told everyone that God was going to destroy the whole world with a flood, but no one believed him. Poor Noah! He preached for years and years while he built the Ark, but his neighbors only laughed at him (II Peter 2:5).

When the Flood did come, only his own family was saved. All of the other people drowned. You see, boys and girls, it is very important to believe God's Word. We can be very thankful that we have God's Word today—the Bible.

Did Dinosaurs Go on Noah's Ark?

God told Noah that some of *every* kind of land animal would come onto the Ark (Genesis 6:19). Did God tell Noah *not* to take dinosaurs on board? No, so they must have been there, too.

I am sure you have a very important question to ask. How did Noah fit all these big monsters on the Ark?

Well, first of all, I do not think God would have brought the biggest, oldest dinosaurs on the Ark. He probably sent strong, young ones that would have babies after the Flood. Remember that many dinosaurs were not very large when they were grown, and all of them were small when they were young.

Secondly, although there are many different dinosaur names, there may have been fewer than fifty kinds of dinosaurs. Creation scientists from ICR have shown that there was plenty of room in the Ark for all the kinds of animals God sent to Noah.

Why Do We Find Fossil Dinosaurs?

This is a very sad picture. All the sinful people that did not go on the Ark drowned. The whole world and even all the land animals were destroyed as God punished those sinful people. Only those that were on the Ark were saved (Genesis 7:23).

Today, people still sin, don't they? All of us sin sometimes (Romans 3:23), and the Bible says God still punishes sinful people. But, we don't need the Ark to save us. God sent the Lord Jesus Christ to die on the cross for our sins (Romans 5:8). Jesus was punished instead of us. If we tell Him we are sorry for the wrong things we have done, He promises to forgive us, and make us His own children. He promises to help us not sin anymore, and we will live with Him forever.

What would you expect to find all over the earth after the Flood
waters ripped up tons of soil and rock and drowned all those
animals and people? You know what I think? I think you would
expect to find billions of dead things buried in rock layers, laid
down by water, all over the earth. And, that is exactly what you
find! Billions (that means lots and lots) of dead things, which have
now changed into fossils: fossil shells, fossil frogs, fossil fish, and,
I am sure you can guess, fossil dinosaurs. This is where dinosaur
fossils come from. They were some of the animals that died in
Noah's Flood. All of the dinosaurs not inside Noah's Ark drowned.
Now we can only see their fossils.

25

PART 3
DINOSAURS AFTER THE FLOOD

After about five months, the Flood waters began to go down and Noah's Ark landed. When the land began to dry out, the plants started to grow again. After six more months, Noah, his family and the animals left the Ark. Noah built an altar to thank God for keeping them safe during the Flood. The dinosaurs and other animals that were on the Ark left as soon as the Flood was over. God told them to live in all parts of the earth. Sometimes they had to walk a long way to find food to eat and start a new home. But soon there were animals all over the earth again.

Do you know the name of the mountain that the Ark landed on? Mount Ararat. Don't you wish you could go to Mount Ararat and see if the Ark is still there? Some people think it still is. I hope somebody finds it one day.

What do you see in the sky just above the mountain? A beautiful rainbow! God put a rainbow in the sky after the Flood, and promised that He would never again send another flood like Noah's Flood.

27

What Happened to the Dinosaurs?

After the Flood, the world was not as nice as it once was. The air was cloudy and dusty from volcanoes. There were hot deserts and places with ice and snow. It was not as easy to live in this world that had been changed by the Flood. Some of the big dinosaurs must have been big eaters. Scientists think that Apatosaurus would have eaten up to 2000 pounds of plants each day. Since the Flood had destroyed all the forests, it was hard for them to get enough good food to live.

Most of the dinosaurs were not able to stay alive in this new world. Poor D. J.—he looks sad, doesn't he? If Adam had not sinned, this would not have happened. Every time we see or think about death, we should be reminded of our sin. But, isn't it wonderful that Jesus came and died on the Cross and rose again from the dead so our sins can be forgiven?

Can you think of other reasons why dinosaurs may have all died? ICR scientists think the Ice Age, a time when much of the world was covered with ice, came after the Flood. Since dinosaurs were probably reptiles, maybe it was just too cold for them. Maybe their favorite plants no longer grew. Perhaps packs of large animals killed the dinosaurs, or small ones ate their eggs. Maybe the air was different. We just don't know all the things that could have happened. But we do know that lots of other animals, not just dinosaurs, have also all died since the Flood. Can you name any of these other animals? This might be an interesting project for you and your family to do at the library. I can think of mammoths and sabre-tooth tigers. I'm sure you can think of others, too.

What do you think this knight is about to do? Yes, kill a dinosaur. It is very possible some dinosaurs were killed by hunters. Perhaps stories like "St. George and the Dragon" are really true stories of someone killing a monster like a dinosaur. For all these reasons, it seems that all (or almost all) of the dinosaurs are now dead.

29

Will We Ever See a Live Dinosaur?

Well. . .maybe. There are some scientists who think there may be a real live dinosaur living in a dark jungle in Africa. If we found one, I would love to bring it back and put on a show at ICR.

Well, boys and girls, at another time D. J. and I may be able to tell you many other things about Creation and the Flood, but we've run out of room. Meanwhile, to find out more about God's wonderful Creation, why don't you and your parents read Genesis, chapters one and two, which tell us about the Creation, and chapters seven through nine, which tell us about the Flood. Bye for now. We hope to see you again for more Creation adventures.